For Mum & Dad

Ping!

 CB

Poems by Iain Whiteley

Write Bloody UK

www.writebloodyuk.co.uk

First edition.
ISBN: 978-1-8380332-1-7

Cover Design by Luna aït Oumeghar
Interior Layout by Winona León
Edited by Fern Angel Beattie

Type set in Bergamo.

Write Bloody UK
London, UK

Support Independent Presses
writebloodyuk.co.uk

PING!

Ping!

Pong 13

of never being chosen. 14

Filesharing 1987 15

More Reissues Than Vogue (Vogue! Vogue! Vogue!) 16

eurovision party 17

Protection 18

Ghazal Like 19

On Scaffolding 20

Pretty Brutal 21

How Are You Getting There? 22

Like Whitney Sang, the Children Are Our Future
and if You Don't Have Those, Get Lost. 23

Claustrophile 24

files 25

Browsers 26

The Singularity 27

Proposal for a Grammarly Plug-in 28

Cybohemians 29

Once We Were Vikings 30

On the Eurostar 31

In Wuppertal 33

City Break 34

Nuts 35

Private View 36

The Slaves of Solitude 37

Off-Menu 38

The Rats of 214 Oxford Street 40

Mankle 42

Inappropriately Dressed 43

milks (oat) 44

milks (soy) 45

milks (cow) 46

Notes on a Big Fat Crisis 47

Subliminal 48

Clarification 49

Miss Great Britain's Great Migration 50

SCHAFERNAKER'S HAIR I 51
SCHAFERNAKER'S HAIR II 51
WE'RE STRAVAIGING 52
SUBLET 53
DEEP CLEANSE 54
EVERYONE ELSE: 55
DISCO, OWL! 56
NEW ZEALAND VARIANT 57
CORNISH TIPSY 58
RAVE FOR ONE 59
MEDITATION 60
CYCLING TO OUTCAST 62
PANTOUM IN AUTUMN 63
PING! 64

NOTES 67
ACKNOWLEDGEMENTS 71

Bloop

blip

so

hip

pro-

to

joy

stick

2

D

line

trip

all

night

PONG

OF NEVER BEING CHOSEN.

cold sticks to you like morning bacon
smells on a winter uniform little milk-knees
knock your face in I will keep your
face down look at the grass mixes with
mud mixes with chalk-line sludge little
biscuits dunked in tea what I wouldn't give
to be at home with you else what
just 90 more minutes of shit kicked in waiting
on the line exposed you will look back at
this will explain a few things nothing
like that feeling of never being chosen.

Filesharing 1987

At playtime we meet in the cloakroom
by the temporary classroom
which is against the rules
and smells of PVA glue.

He shields his eyes from the sunshine
hands me Axel F in a Woolworth's bag
takes 6 minutes 32 seconds of Mel & Kim
and after 3.30pm
we get fresh in our rooms playing records.

I like him
because everyone else prefers tapes
and his dad's 47
like my dad's 47
which is embarrassing
because the other dads
are young like Morten Harket

who my sister loves
but I don't
because I'm a boy
and boys can't love Morten Harket.

MORE REISSUES THAN VOGUE
(VOGUE! VOGUE! VOGUE!)

Next time, I'm arriving in a picture sleeve with 3 new mixes and a fabulous badge

my functional traits (*name, length, producers*) painted sexy in kanji, wrapped in an obi

every conquest etched on my neck (now a heavyweight imprint, not fly-by-night flexi or god forbid shellac)

I'll have a spine, an advisory sticker to sell copies of me quicker, a glossy coat you'll want to sniff

I am layered, angular, deep

.devil the summon I'll backwards me Play

EUROVISION PARTY

remember the production values
of that eurovision night?
such insane production values!
you spent nine pounds
on a sixties drinks cabinet
from the dead people's shop round the corner
and we filled the stolen ice bucket

onstage were heels
huge, sparkling things
under fishnetted prosthetics
that spread wider
– so much wider! –
than that tiny front roomful
of manchester queens

and as the limbs parted
an ex-spice girl
dangled unseductively
where the knickers should be
flanked by tan-oiled hulks
with stomachs tighter
than that bitch at moss side job centre

glittering streamers
rained from the stage
while georgia gave russia
douze points again
and i wonder, still wonder
did we accidentally drop acid
in our spumante cocktails
instead of angostura bitters?

PROTECTION

They are in a box my angel past the crystals. You must go down a narrow ginnel (purple cloaks the door). The room will smell of amyl walk to the back. Feel your face burn. Your head will bang the woman will stare everyone knows. Pick up that box you damn well pick it up you damn well pay for it. Find five little dolls inside. Put these in your pocket they will protect you from the outside they will keep their eyes on you.

GHAZAL LIKE

Don't thrust your way of talking upon us like.
Our speech is a marker among us like.

Does received wisdom iron out imperfections?
More shame if our dialects are goners like.

Your scorn won't round out my flat vowels.
I can still pass linguistics with honours like.

Estuary or Queen's don't guarantee brains.
But what would we know? We're commoners like.

Racism's the same in any accent.
Your prejudice is on you, not on us like.

One isn't lazy or simple or stupid;
one feels *reet at yam* in this tongue, one does like.

---

reet at yam: right at home (Cumbrian dialect)

On Scaffolding

Yeah, you don't wanna mess with scaffolders
when they're done working on your property.
Might be an accident with your winders.

Sorry though, love – it ain't to do with me.
It must be a right pain I imagine,
but I'm only paid to fix the roof, see.

I'm not saying they're thugs or anything,
or that they're chancers taking advantage
– some of my best mates work in scaffolding –

but you might find you're used for free storage,
which could be why they've left it on your house.
They don't really stick to that old adage,

you know, about what goes up must come down?
With public land, the council's like a rash:
all over 'em. But this? You're on your own.

I could ask my mates to help. They take cash.

PRETTY BRUTAL The fortress that is the Brutalist Appreciation Society imposes absolute restrictions on the particular buildings its members can admire. Those who dare suggest a Letňany panelak or a Dresdner plattenbau are to be enjoyed within said collective's stark four walls are very much mistaken. Any building as machine-for-waiting must never be fetishized. Apprentices may not wait at Soviet bus stops, or may wait but wait in perpetuity. These purists won't stop there. NOT BRUTALIST they holler from Bulgarian water towers. The uninitiated will be crushed. (Polite diktat: membership is not – mon dieu! – defined by brutish traits.) Need a rest? Feast on aesthetic sanitoria in desolate locations. Looking for sympathy? Try the Postmodern Appreciation Society. Now, let's get to the Corbusier of the problem. It's Erich Honecker's new clothes. I mean: have you seen Preston bus station in the rain? Raw is not the word.

How Are You Getting There?

Car people follow
hearts & train people
follow tracks.

Car people skip
waiting at the train
station to free-

wheel the moonscape.
Train people dream
of juggernauting

volcanic terrain but
actually, we hire carriages
on extremely terrifying

rollercoasters, scramble
for the front wagon,
raise our hands to loop-

the-loop, kid ourselves
that one day, maybe,
we'll crash out the funfair

– like car people do.

Like Whitney Sang, the Children Are Our Future and if You Don't Have Those, Get Lost.

Of the rest, Lords and Business Men are most important, followed by (medical) doctors and professional footballers. These can sleep together in Business Class. Some footballers are handsome and all doctors are handsome, especially gay doctors. Surgeons are the most handsome doctors and gay surgeons are the most handsome doctors. The most handsome gay surgeons went to Oxbridge.

No footballers are gay but gay doctors (excluding pre-registration) can sometimes sleep in Business Class. This is occasionally true for (straight-acting) business gays although business gays are rare. I do not know about women. Business lesbians are similar to business gays. They are not so rare and you demarcate them using the smoking-divider curtain from a heyday 747. When their business fails, gays up to 40 make excellent cabin crew. Lesbians (any age) can be highly effective mechanics.

CLAUSTROPHILE

Back in the car years,
hunting the world in packs,
before everyone did their first Noah
and paired off to the ark,
we drove round town:
two up front; three
or four back seat drivers;
you, stuffed in the boot,
or trunk for the Yanks

who also say shotgun
– the prime spot for every young punk
apart from you, who craved the safety
of enclosed spaces,
laughed in the face of statistics,
and found comfort in breaking
the law so blatantly

undercover. On our roads to nowhere,
you lived for surprising humps,
smashed your head,
which invariably led to muffled concerns
through padded partitions
about dents in cars.

You loved it: being locked away,
simultaneously centre of attention,
much like the murder victim
of this Netflix drama;
oxygen-starved in the back
of her car in a Belfast forest,
which brings me to think of you now;

how you might be;
what you do for middle-aged kicks;
if you're driven these days
to squat in your John Lewis wardrobe,
close the door and gently rock.

FILES

mpeg jpeg mp3
tiff doc gif zip ftp
xml wav svg
pdf http

BROWSERS

– after CSS Francine

This waxy Renaissance beauty
confirms what I have long
suspected: no man is a flat pixel
and we cannot be saved
as files. We are pure
code – each of us line
after line of hypertext
and style sheets
at the mercy of others'
browsers. Who programs us
is a bigger question of course
and one no Chrome
nor Opera can render.
The big script kid in the sky?
A million virtual monkeys?
Whatever. The point is this:
we can tweak our perfect code;
people read us as they will.

THE SINGULARITY

I am not a robot.
I am not a robot.
I am not a robot.
I am not a robot.
I am not a robot.
I am not a robot.
I am not a robot.
I am not a robot.
I am not a robot.
I am not a robot.
I am not a robot.
I am not a robot.
I am not a robot.
I am not a robot.
I am not a robot.
I am not a robot.
I am not a robot.
I am not a robot.
I am not a robot.
I am not a robot.
I am not a robot.
I am not a robot.
I am not a robot.
I am not a robot.
I am not a robot.
I am not a robot.
I am not a robot.
I am not a robot.
I am not a robot.
I am not a
I am
I
am
a
robot.

Proposal for a Grammarly Plug-in

Guys, as apprentice writer, I recall being chastised by my old-school editor for checking out verbs on my smartphone. The man was a lover of tradition; of wordbooks; of doing things properly – mistakenly assuming me to be googling my grammar. Even he, however, could not fail to be impressed when I showed him the Collins-red portal, which not only hosted more synonyms than his dusty two-volumed old-faithfuls but also offered regular updates, contexts and sounds.

He's six feet under now of course, his dictionaries decomposing, his only remaining works ink-jetted pink on the purple backs of non-compostable chocolate wrappers, but I often consider what he would make of your excellent linguistic tool, which I use to appear clear, correct and uniform with every form of my written word, including now, as I write with news of my own application, under development, which harnesses your technology, and encapsulates elements of face- and auto-tune, beloved of influencers and popstars respectively, though not exclusively, to provide speakers as well as writers with a thoroughly consistent voice, devoid of hesitation or clunky syntactic error, in real-time, and for time immemorial (or until their subscription is cancelled, whichever is sooner).

My proposed widget, currently in beta, is a thorax plug-in, nestling neatly and discretely between the vocal chords, by means of tracheotomy, utilising, as per your current tool, a series of predefined rules to ensure plosives, fricatives and other such phonemes hit specified vernacular goals. It niftily ranks utterances in real time, measuring sensitivity, verbosity, accuracy and so on, amending and deleting as necessary (admittedly requiring a large listening-in team initially, but ultimately carried out by machine). The prototype's ready and I am currently working to enlist an assistant, so if you know someone willing, could you give me a shout by return? I have a surgeon who is desperate to operate.

CYBOHEMIANS

こんにちは/Konnichiwa David!
Your grey curls are flowing today!
You are, doubtless, the finest
Renaissance statue to surf
our cherry-blossom chessboard.
Which move next?
Across—forward—back?
Don't worry how you travel;
just take our elevator!
We play lift muzak,
produced by vagabonds
—cybohemians,
vapor-waving goodbye
to aesthetic meaning,
burning towards an 8-bit sunrise
as it floods the Windows 95
of our fifth floor apartment.
We're in Miami, Japan,
or a sex hotel near Incheon,
playing our lives to death;
we could be in the Highlands
—you'll never know,
because where we live,
it's Guy Fawkes every night.

Once We Were Vikings

gorging ourselves
on cow, hen and pig
 gnawed straight from the bone
sprawled on wood benches
 in nicotine caves
drowning and belching down
 tankards of ale
as summer-job wenches
 flashed us their knickers
and you grabbed my crotch
 as we chain-smoked through courses
we axed through new countries
 spilled blood, sweat and semen
on walls, doors and carpets
 ran wild through night-houses
slept on the streets
 traded culture
language
 whiskey and anger
swung from the laughter
 of youth, love and danger
untouched by our future
 just now ever after

ON THE EUROSTAR

Brussels is empty. Do not travel to Brussels. The suspect remains at large. A major attack is planned. Helicopter is flying low the malls are shuttered. He might .have a suicide belt I am your train manager. Avoid high highly highly highly crowded areas. Stay vigilant. Respect security checks. There is a chance of weapons. He is hiding. His brother blew himself. up Visit Café Metropole. Do not take public transport. I am your train manager. Stations remain closed soldiers. Patrol the streets. This is getting the terror. Brussels is in grave danger. It is a melange of cultures. This train runs under the sea. A suspect is on the run. The army is on the street. The terror is in Brussels. This is an attack. This train is for Brussels. Avoid Brussels. This train is for Brussels. Do not travel do not travel travel to Brussels. This train is nonstop. To Brussels. Follow the advice of authorities. He is hiding in the Bruss under the sea. A suspect els area. It is an ongoing incident. Brussels is closed. A police helicopter is flying low. The malls are shuttered. HE MIGHT T HAVE A SUICIDE BELT He might have a suicide belt. I am your train manager. Avoid highly highly highly crowded areas. Stay vigilant. Respect security checks. There is a chance of weapons. He is hiding. checks. there his brother blew himself. up Visit Café Metropole. Do not take public transport. grave danger. I am your train manager. Stations remain closed. Soldiers patrol the streets. This is getting serious. The city centre is a military base. Thank you for travelling with Eurostar. THERE IS A CHANCE A chance of weapons. explosives. Security has been stepped up. Attacks from chemical. very serious. weapons are possible. We wish you a pleasant journey. Terror level four. Brussels is under helicopter is flying low. The malls are shuttered. He might have a suicide belt. I am your train manager grave grave threat. a grave threat. Avoid highly crowded highly crowded areas. Stay vigilant. Respect security checks. There is a chance of weapons. He is hiding. His brother blew himself. up Visit Café Metropole. Do not take public transport. I am your train TERROR or manager. Stations remain closed. He might have a suicide belt soldiers patrol the streets. His brother blew himself. up This is getting major attack. Nonstop. A major attack is planned. The terro we have no firm information. At least one attack. er is in Belgium. under the sea. A suspect shelter in place. REMAIN AT HOME Remain at home! his train will arrive on time. Biological weapons may be used. There is a terrorist arsenal in Brussels. Security has been stepped up. Several individuals may be armed with explosives. An attack could be launched. The situation is serious. THIS IS SERIOUS. This is getting serious.panic. The situation is monitored permanently. Follow the advice of authorities. The interior ministry has published an infographic. This is very serious. Do not do not give in to panic. Avoid areas with high footfall. Order a Belgian waffle. Attacks are. Attacks are possible. This is a co-ordinated attack. Thank ordinated co-ordinated attack. Thank co-ordinated attack. Thank ordinated attack. Thank you for travelling with Eurostar. The terrorist is at large We must be very attentive. A major attack is planned. Alert level is high. We wish you a safe onward journey. Alert level This is serious. Several terrorists are at large. We face a grave threat. Thank you for travelling with Eurostar. This is getting serious. This is very dangerous. I am your train manager. The metro is suspended. We will shortly be arriving in Brussels. This is very serious. A major attack is planned.

In Wuppertal

We snake along the river, dangling.
A steely dance above the rain-soaked trees.
Below, *die Fabrik* built on heroin.
We snake along the river. Dangling.
We hang on every wheel's electric spin.
Our *Kaiserwagen* glides among the green.
We snake along – the river dangling.
A steely dance. Above, the rain-soaked trees.

CITY BREAK

Bare *katzenjammered*
a night off the rails
he is stock-market crashed
at risk in the *Grunewald*
quantitatively, uneased

Rinsed economically
his D
     N
         An unravelled commodity
he is searching for *Alex*
a bed of his own
a train back to dignity
home

NUTS

This room is nuts. Nuts fireplace,
nuts picture frames, nuts walls.
Walls of orange Anaglypta. Nuts.

This house is nuts. Nuts cornicing,
nuts layout, nuts carpet.
Carpet in the bathroom. Nuts.

This street is nuts. Nuts streetlamps,
nuts speedbumps, nuts neighbours.
Neighbours with a nutty dog. Called Nuts.

This town is nuts. Nuts locals,
nuts one-way system, nuts bridges.
Cantilever, suspension, beam (all nuts).

This country's nuts:
nuts artists, nuts academics,
nuts doctors working nuts hours

in a nuts world with a nuts climate,
filled with nuts wildlife and
nuts oceans we've barely explored. Nuts!

This universe is nuts! Nuts nebulae,
nuts galaxies, nuts black holes.
Black holes that swallow stars

Private View

I'm hit by your walls,
too naïve to know a Klee from a Burra.
Then, despite your failing lungs,
you boom at me: speak clearly,

with clarity, would I like whisky?
In the taxi, you say you'd
get on well with my father,
though respectfully, I disagree:

he's no raconteur and nor am I,
a fact instantly recognised
by the artist, who is not happy
with your choice of guest. She

turns her head from her cigarette,
skims me like grit. Tragically,
I dip my eyes to the Mayfair floor,
wince at the mess of it. You laugh,

insist you introduce me anyway,
take a long drag of Marlboro
and – in this lightbulb moment! –
I'm cropped from the front page.

THE SLAVES OF SOLITUDE

Our theatre is housed
between carved-up villas
on a tree-lined avenue
where maids of all work

once fussed over middle
classes. At interval drinks,
two men from the front
row finalise a Park Lane

sale and shake on a cool
six million. I think of your
sadness; how it hangs
in the flat where a picture

could be. Neat walls.
Pristine floors. A closet.
Those clothes piled
on top of your dreams.

OFF–MENU

Whispering couples
feel awkward

with our
breach of

societal norms.
Seems to

them, we
hang around

like a
crap party,

spoil the
fun, force

lovers to
avert their

gaze, especially
on Fridays

when waiters
are also

not fans.
Solo diners

hog valuable
space at

the table
— *no sir,*

that's fine —
the fine

being sat
by the

bins. In
the city,

it's easy,
almost a

hobby, dining
alone: why

go home
with such

elaborate choice
and so

many mouths
to offend?

Itadaki Zen!
Franco Manca!

Andy's Greek
Taverna! They

are ours
for the

taking – if
we leave

sharing platters
aside.

The Rats of 214 Oxford Street

i.m. Big Topshop (1994 -2021)

It was always so tricky in that building.
Handy for harbourage and every convenience,
but it was the noise – those blasted DJs
spinning house from 10 till 10
and later on launch nights, and even then
there was no peace: cleaners, stockists, visual
merchandisers fussing till first tube,
which was why, from Britpop to Brexit,
they huddled in cavity walls and ceilings,
breeding and feeding and hiding and thieving
till everything stopped overnight.
Everyone just vanished
and they couldn't put their claws on why.
Still, the quiet flushed them out
to this six-tier explosion of suedette,
neon and impossibly chiselled mannequins,
which were first to get weed on.
They ratted the hair salon
on the lower ground floor;
dip-dyed their whiskers; span round
in barber chairs; sugared their ratty brows.
Across the way, they raticured nails
in rose-gold and mint,
left trails as they skittered the stairs.
In menswear, they savaged
spray-on jeans, took one leg per tail,
got grillz for their front incisors.
The stupid ones pierced their tongues.
Word got round, and as the bins
on Oxford Street emptied, neighbours
all the way to Regent Street Cinema
joined the throngs of *Rattus Fashionistus*
gnawing cute tubs of frosting,
tapioca bubbles and endless racks of leather.

This was the flagship of all ratships:
ninety-thousand square feet of overconsumption,
feasting on the fabric of slave labour
and falling apart at the seams.
Conditions became unsanitary,
the building unsafe
and Boss Rat scuttled off with their pensions.
Yet on they gnawed and writhed
and chewed through straps and shoes,
fabrics, manbags,
crazed and ravenous, unable to stop,
unwilling, spilling through doors, windows, floors,
to Bond Street, South Molton,
Mayfair, the sewers below

MANKLE

Your three quarter
length trouser stirs

an interest in mine;
so funny, this bone

now an erogenous
zone to me and

half of Essex. Central
London's moved on

to wide legs or shorts
with sports socks,

but here you are,
still teasing my eyes

with this macho
flash of flesh.

INAPPROPRIATELY DRESSED

I wake up feeling remarkably gay
so I pop to Waitrose in my Uggs. I'm
not wearing anything apart from Uggs
so by the time I get to the entrance
and the police are called, I'm making
a pass at them. They ask me if I like
Belinda Carlisle to which I respond
yes, I like anyone with a surname
from the county of my birth and
anyway have they tried reading a
poem called *I fucking hate Belinda
Carlisle* to a middle-aged poetry class?
If so, they would know it results in
the rigmarole of explaining
that just because a poem's been written,
it doesn't mean it's actually true,
which though the class nod, clearly
goes only a partial way to abating their
mistrust. Anyway, the feds nod
and log a report in the present perfect
and let me off with a caution. I only want
some Duchy eggs as it happens, the blue
ones, which is why I've come here and not
Lidl. The rest of the trip passes without
fanfare and I enjoy the wolf whistles
although not the one guy who tells me
I'm asking for it. Things only get weird
when I scan the eggs, because I'm expecting
to be told about the unexpected items in
my bagging area and instead the lady with
the cheery user-tested robot voice informs
me that my Uggs are actually slippers?

MILKS (OAT)

golden barley fields:
rain-plumped, de-husked & rebirthed.
porridge for coffee

MILKS (SOY)

sprawling cerrado
– lost to deforestation
and curdled hot drinks

MILKS (COW)

what to do today?
munch grass – let supermarkets
squeeze teats & profits

Notes on a Big Fat Crisis

re: crisis in the spreads aisle

Turns out it's spreading? (Consumers not buying it)

No carbs before Marbs = no marge either

Trans fats = kill people or something?

Shoppers want their fat natural/not hydrogenated

If we don't act fast, our prestigious client = <u>a thing of the past</u>

Bottom line: WE NEED TO SELL MORE **FAT**

Question: **how do we do that?**

- half the country on a diet that we are promoting

- other half only eat McDonald's (also us – great campaign)

Packaging: use brown plastic (looks eco)/
make strapline scream *"EAT CLEAN!"*

????influencers

<u>NEED A TIE-IN.</u>

Veganuary = a mouthful   (also market saturated)

Global warming MASSIVE. Can we sponsor that?

SUBLIMINAL

Are you a writer looking for
connotations of half-truths,
deception, outright fraud,
vanity, fear, snobbery, false
pride and radio programmes
hideous with wheedling voices?
Well you've come to the right
place because poetry is
part of everyday life and
it's best enjoyed when
laughed over, thought about
and acted upon by multitudes.
You can increase saleability
of your poems by making
them reminiscent of gaiety,
romance and aristocratic
elegance (or symbolic of
tragedy or suggestive of
glowing health and youth
– depending on your whim).
Poets can invite readers to
make identifications of
themselves in new roles, so
let's try that now, as you take
on your new character of
"smart housewife and hostess
(who deserves Spam)."

Adapted from the article:
Poetry and Advertising by S.I Hayakawa in POETRY magazine vol 67, no. 4 (Jan 1946) p.204

CLARIFICATION

"Our dictionaries reflect rather than dictate
how language is used. This is driven solely
by evidence of how real people use English
in their daily lives."

– Oxford University Press

To misspeak *(verb)*: grow a nose;
blow ducks; cook the books;
take for a ride; throw cream in the eyes;
tell salads; roll in flour; hang noodles;
yank the chain; sell a lemon; sell snake oil;
sell a pup; tell a whopper; wear a cat;
talk hot mash; lead up the garden path-
ological; keep horizontal; stretch;
bend; manipulate; exaggerate; fabricate;
disinformate. To clarify: *mon œil*.

Miss Great Britain's Great Migration

All the world's a revolution
Miss Great Britain's no exception

orchestrates her new beginning
spins the string-bass, whirls the organ.

Ball gown blurs the Winter Gardens
trips the summer night fantastic

esplanades the deckchair flotsam
promenades the catwalk pier.

Washboard skiffles! Whips a frenzy!
Jettisons her whoops-a-daisies!

Dons a vest of weighted cockles:
Carry On ~*sploosh*~ Rule Britannia.

Schafernaker's Hair I

Never mind Schrödinger: this guy's a redhead whether the cat lives or dies.
No paradox.
But what about his bloody barnet?
Isn't it just weird?!?!
Now hang on.
If a man can be both Zeus and un-preened,
his response at the same time angry and coy *(wink!)*,
will your nasty tweet still exist, and not, when you delete it?

Schafernaker's Hair II

Speaking of quantum entanglement, the only guy to ever love me
calls me his ginger cutie, which he does to wind me up because I'm
emotionally unavailable. He thinks I get angry because I don't want to
be ginger, but who doesn't want to be ginger? I get angry because I'm
not ginger. I get angry because I'm not ginger and tell him: *I'm not angry*
with you because I don't want to be ginger, I'm angry with you because I'm not
ginger. Who doesn't want to be ginger? I'd give anything to have Schafernaker's
hair. What I really mean here is: *I'd give my right weather vane to have*
Schafernaker's smooth chest/artistic merit/sex appeal/job/cultural capital/
patience on social media/abs/respect for law/friends/skin tone/wealth/popularity/
garden furniture. My unrequited lover toys with thought experiments:
This man both loves me, and does not; we are both couple, and not. And me?
I'm thinking of my beautiful friend Angus, who insists he's not ginger
and is red as a Highland cow.

WE'RE STRAVAIGING

and the sun doorways the sky.

We camber out-

side: plankton   expelled from the mouth of Momma

Barnacle.

       Just look at us! We're a right pair

of larvae-at-larges

     – brimming with diminished intention and zero wherewithal

to glue our feet – ever – on rocks

                ships

                 or blubber.

We unravel the day:

     catch it on parks   benches   trees

but mostly bars.

We amble early   while the world rears its young.

     Cheers!

         to innocence lost

       to time

   friendship

        the magic of hanging

Sublet

And in this world my worktop and industrial lamp
feel inconsequential, the belongings of a young
couple, the son of a Polish success, the great
granddaughter of a Jewish maid, and here they are,
come good with this elegant space in Govan and me,
all Lady Macbeth, tarnishing the woodgrain in the
kitchen of the place they say I'll love for its retro
furniture, him filtered and Instagram-ready, not
in that moment knowing me bunkered away from death,
lies, asphyxiation, injustice, all my anger
directed at the wine stain, rubbing till it's chafed,
furious, blistered, a scuff-marked disaster of my own
making, the difference being that I will admit
to this, pay for it, offer contrition like herbal
bitters, never deny in the face of all fact and
truth, not like nasty bastards, blusters of privilege,
cheating blondes, grotesque hypocrites, evidence twisters,
public fictioneers, plinth-clutching shit-speakers, brazen
liars, shameless, *questions create questions*, denial,
move on, refusal, rebuke, silly boy, well I can
be a narcissist too you murderers, I can say
yes, behold my legacy, here on this worktop, me.

DEEP CLEANSE

here she is with her New Zealand blood, back from a do with
Alec Baldwin, getting shouted at by Gregory for leaving her cups on
the sideboard *you should do some life drawing* she shouts back *it's good
for the soul, not that you have one* it's time to turn up the heat so she heads
for the boiler, he grabs her arm, she pulls away, screams *touch me again
I'll call the police, the radiator's bust, I'm nearly 60, I'm tired of being cold for you*
he yells *I'm tired too, tired of this mess, tired from this dry heat, tired of those
fucking gongs you keep ringing, they keep me awake* she looks him straight in
the eye says *Gregory, it's a fucking gong bath, it's frequencies* asks if he
remembers when they were on the same frequency, he's shaking,
tells her it's torture, he doesn't care what kind of bath it is, it's like
waterboarding, *living with you is like fucking waterboarding, the vibrations
make me crazy* she laughs, softens, tells him he's always been crazy, asks
how the gongs are on his bowels *because sometimes they give me the runs*

EVERYONE ELSE:

me: can u entertain me plz / i don't wanna be here / i wish it was the early 80s & i was going to the blitz nightclub & i lived in a squat / the subjunctive is so over / if you don't reply i'll just keep talking / hello / all i can think about is the camden town-east village ripped up a–z cover of borderline circa 1983 / on another note but in a similar vein i don't really mind if i am in a squat in london & going to the blitz or if i am in a squat in new york & going to the danceteria / either or really / would i have been sade or boy george / i can't decide / depends who gets more beards / did they have beards then / i prefer sade's songs / the jury's out / can u get me a time machine so i can check / i'll be the 18-year-old living in a squat in the early 80s / can i be steve strange / is fade to grey cooler / will rusty egan do a mix / will u sign me to sire records / let's hang out with sonic youth / i wanna sleep rough in st mark's square near the bookshop / get real famous /go to Studio 54 / or is that the 70s / they def had beards then / can u transport me to the west coast / i'll weave flowers in my hair / make mama cass all healthy / i'm not being fattist / i'll buy her a soda / we can duet / in harmony / it would be even better than the real thing / o no that's U2

Disco, Owl!

I'd like to disco
but being merely an owl
I only barn dance

New Zealand Variant

J. M Barrie literally named you. On the best days, you are saturated with colour: a vivid la Chapelle. You are Westwood's shoe when Naomi's ankle gives way. The supermodel smile that follows. You are sunglasses at night. Coco. And chenille. You are a fashion shoot – on film, of course – and your supporting models – seven disgracefully handsome Gaultier sailors – will become obsessed with you, follow you afterwards, chirp-chirping like Disney birds to a chi-chi bar in South Pigalle, return home five days later. Hangovers excepted, you do not have bad days. You do have Cruella's bark though. And balayage. Your hangovers are Jackson Pollock. Sometimes, you wear a fake arse for breakfast. You built a nebula in the living room. And a throne of hair. We went to Studio 54. You taught me things. *The most important people always leave, but their memory never fades.* Your brain interferes with the electrics. Sometimes it is too much. A decade on, I can still read you like a book I haven't read. Do you remember when we climbed inside the mannequins? There is adventure in your eyes. It is terrifying. And magnificent. That's pure art, you say. That's terrible. That's shocking. You laugh your wicked laugh. Do you remember spying on the neighbours? We laughed so loud and so hard and so fierce that they heard through two lots of double glazing and a main road and moved out. You have a faulty connection. You're a wind-up drumming monkey. Your laugh is looped, stretched and overdubbed. It is spliced and pitch-adjusted. You know how to laugh. You ignore unnecessary importance. You filter details that matter. You are Light Lady, by which I don't mean you light up people's lives, I mean you make costumes out of lights. You light up people's lives. You are roof down, jungle tunes up, bringing the milkshake. You belong in the Louvre (but would break yourself out). You choose adventure over security, and you mostly don't regret it. Exquisite eye. Haywire woman! Fire raging.

Cornish Tipsy

(i)
Ou sont les cigarettes, I thought they said at art school, but when I got to art school they said *Don't paint from photographs*, which was odd, because I was studying drama.

(ii)
You can't make sense of heartbreak was my flatmate's mantra. I thought my flatmate sounded depressed but it could have been his accent. For three years, he meticulously painted a sheet of white[1] on a background of white on a canvas of white. Sometimes the sheet was curly. Sometimes the sheet was ripped. Sometimes the sheet was folded.

(iii)
I developed a drink problem and a love of roast potatoes. Each night I got violently tipsy and stumbled into a roast potato shop selling limp roast potatoes with tough skins. I'd leave, shouting at the roast potatoes, telling them how much I loved them and smearing mayonnaise all over my body. This stopped me forming meaningful relationships, which is a skill I retain.

(d)
Let me in I need a pasty, I screamed. *A chicken one.* (This happened in the local Spa not the roast potato shop.) I was slurring about how all my friends were artists and writers and not lawyers or bankers or medics, not like before. The woman gave me the pasty and told me it wasn't right, thousands of students in one small town, she remembered before we came there were fewer marijuanas.

---

1 It is possible my flatmate was inspired by Kazimir Malevich's 1918 painting *White on White* in which a white square floats weightlessly in a white field – a geometric abstraction with no reference to external reality; however, more research is needed.

Rave for One

I only think *quarry* because I think of the slate
mines at Coniston, but this is not smiley-face bracken
and caves; it's a natural amphitheatre with a small,
stage-level opening. To get here, take a sharp
right from the gate and make an entrance
through leaves. A surround-sound of steep,
mossy gradient confronts me: a branchy coven
on top; roots ripple downward like soundwaves.
It's chilly this early and I can taste the sea
but can't see it from my woodland womb.
Twigs and dry fern flank my tiny mountain grove
and I collect them for burning. I sit by the fire
on a natural limestone patio. A little litter.
Not much – just enough to feel romantic.
A cider bottle. Cigarette ends. Teenagers probably,
or a lazy kindred spirit. It's not the hour for alcohol,
and anyway, mine is not that kind of party. I pour coffee
from a flask. Flames strobe the withering darkness.
Gulls circle a pylon-buzz. I contemplate
sheep: how they pissed themselves in the 90s,
but these days seem fearless. I put on headphones.
Pulse with rhythm. Take to my floor, and dance
like nobody's watching. Trees fractal a molten sky.
Daylight gurns euphoric. I lift my arms
to red squelch, acid morning.

MEDITATION

I take my state-approved exercise,
head past the *gompa*, stomp the coastline
woods of golden mulch, yellow leaves,
my feet browning like gravy browning
to a clearing in the trees: an open
invitation for runners, walkers,
lovers, to rocky shores and today
is grim, and of course I don't mean the
weather, though of course that is too, and
my eyes, not great at the best of times,
drip with a sweat that's made this contact
lens slip, blurring the dots of the monks'
red robes into pebble-grey beach,
but add to this the spit of rain,
hanging off my lashes, the effect
a lot like freshly sudded windscreens,
right–left–right, not quite see-through-able,
foaming like the very sea behind it,
and if you can imagine all that,
you will get the general picture, but
enough of this, my myopia,
let's get back to those robes on the shore,
because their oranges are really
something, really catch my eye in this
mizzle, a kind of bright I'll remember
well after the event no doubt, and
as I rest to contemplate these holy
beings' being instead of my own
for once, I wonder what it is, that
little white thing they are tending to,
flip-flap flipping in the wind, some kind
of creature I expect, perhaps an
injured seagull they are rescuing,
and my limited knowledge of the
Buddhist tradition has me thinking
they are considering right view, right

action, right intention but as I
squint with my good eye, I see it's chips
in one of those polystyrene trays,
a takeaway, wrapped in white paper,
being mindfully devoured, at which
I turn for home, cheered that life is pure
poetry, and as I do, a
Hercules jet fighter flies low, rips
the sky above the Temple of World Peace.

CYCLING TO OUTCAST

We're cycling to Outcast
on the edge of our town,
your brown hair tied back
under silk and I'm thinking
the shorts you're wearing
are clinging too tight
as they pinch in the flesh
by the mole on your leg.
I'm bouncing
on a canvas seat,
passing fields, horses,
allotments. The herons
are skimming the bay.
Stopping by woods,
we collect catkins
and pinecones,
spot snowdrops
and celandines,
smell perfuming heat
and summering beach.
Arriving at Outcast,
we fill tubs with berries,
avoid the thorns,
and in low autumn sun,
you sing to me
of wild rovers
and bachelor boys.
I see my lonely
future in the lyrics
and in the waxy mirror
of the rosehips.

Pantoum in Autumn

I know how lucky I am,
watching leaves fall from the liquid amber,
the two of you raking and weeding,
rapt in bright autumn days.

Watching leaves fall from the liquid amber,
I remember past Octobers, warmly
wrapped up on bright autumn days.
Now the nights are getting longer,

I remember past Octobers warmly.
I love to watch you in your garden
now. The days are getting shorter
and you are making the most of them.

I love to watch you. In your garden,
you tend to daphne and meadowsweet,
and you are making the most of them.
Together, you are a formidable team.

You tend to jasmine and astilbe.
When they bloom, I will remember you,
together. You make a fastidious team,
preparing the garden for

when it blooms. I will remember you:
the two of you raking and weeding,
preparing the garden. For
I know how lucky I am.

PING!

Now I'm middle-aged

teetering on success

aware my happiest days are numbered

I find myself panicked by your twilight ping! from Hanoi

which pricks like a night call

back when answering was chancing.

You tell me your plans and I'm thirteen again

ringing from a payphone:

I am staying out for pizza.

My shivers now must be the ones you felt then:

I'm eighty, you say

Exactly, I say

How will you cross the road?

You chuckle like gravel.

Tell me it's only Hanoi:

It's good practice, for when I'm further away.

Notes

Pong is a reference to *Pong*, the 1972 tennis videogame created by Atari.

Filesharing 1987 references the song *Axel F* by Harold Faltermeyer, 80s pop duo Mel & Kim, and Morten Harket from Norwegian band A-ha.

An obi, or obi strip, is a paper loop wrapped around vinyl, books and other media in Japan to provide additional information in Japanese.

On Scaffolding was written after reading Simon Armitage's *Very Simply Topping Up the Brake Fluid*.

CSS Francine is an artwork by Diana A. Smith created using only hand-written computer code. When viewed in alternative web browsers, the image is radically altered: diana-adrianne.com video.vice.com/en_ca/video/this-painting-is-made-of-pure-web-code/5b9ad409be40775f7049ff9f

The singularity is the theoretical point in time when technological growth becomes irreversible.

Grammarly is an AI-powered tool to improve written communication: grammarly.com. *Proposal for a Grammarly Plug-in* was written after reading Michael Donaghy's *Poem on the Underground*.

Cybohemians references the 2010s internet microgenre Vaporwave.

Wuppertal is a town in Germany and home to the world's oldest electric elevated railway: schwebebahn.de/en/

The Slaves of Solitude is the name of a 1947 novel by Patrick Hamilton.

214 Oxford Street was the bricks-and-mortar flagship store of Topshop, now an online-only fashion retailer. The poem was inspired by this article about the growing number of rats in London's empty buildings: https://www.theguardian.com/science/2021/feb/07/are-we-losing-the-rat-race-how-rodent-took-over-our-offices

Uggs are Australian footwear.

The saying 'No carbs before Marbs' is attributed to Ellie Redman from TV's *The Only Way is Essex*. It means 'don't eat carbohydrates before going on holiday to Marbella'.

Clarification begins with a quote from Oxford University Press, which can be found in the following article (although the poem does not relate to this article's subject matter in any way): www.theguardian.com/books/2020/nov/07/oxford-university-press-updates-definitions-word-woman

Schafernaker's Hair Part I refers to an incident involving UK meteorologist and presenter Tomasz Schafernaker: chroniclelive.co.uk/news/tv/bbc-tomasz-schafernaker-hair-twitter-18818220

Stravaig is a word of Scottish origin that means to wander.

As well as the named musicians and producers in the poem, *Everyone Else*: refers to three nightclubs from the 70s and 80s (The Blitz, Danceteria, Studio 54).

New Zealand Variant refers to Naomi Campbell's runway malfunction while wearing Vivienne Westwood shoes.

A gompa can loosely be translated as a Buddhist temple or monastery.

Pantoum in Autumn was inspired by multiple readings of Ian Humphreys' poem *Treading Water*.

Acknowledgements

The poems *Sublet, Filesharing 1987* and *of never being chosen.* were first published in the January 2021 edition of *The North* magazine.

Thank you to the following poets whose classes, advice, tutorials or words of wisdom have contributed directly or indirectly to the poems in this book: Susannah Dickey, Leontia Flynn, Nick Laird, Karen McCarthy-Wolfe, Manuela Moser, Daljit Nagra, Katrina Naomi, Maurice Riordan, Padraig Reagan, Richard Scott, Jo Shapcott and Stephen Sexton. Thanks also to my fellow classroom poets for their valuable feedback.

Many of the poems in this collection were written as part of Coffee House Poetry's magnificent online *Between the Lines* courses run by Cahal Dallat. To all the poets on these courses: thanks for your consistently generous critiques and advice. To Cahal: thank you for introducing me to such varied forms and poets, and for doing so with such insight and enthusiasm. Thanks to Anne-Marie Fyfe, also of Coffee House Poetry, for giving me my first-ever stage at The Troubadour in London.

Mega-thanks to Emma Hammond for pushing me further and stopping me from sounding (even more) like a Carry On film. Extra-special thanks to the original, best and never-forgotten English teachers, Jenny Rushton and Jenny Brown. Thanks to Alice Kavounas-Taylor for encouraging me to write poetry – years before I got round to it.

Love and thanks to my readers: Kirsty Kyle for being Angus; Mimi Haddon for taking the lead in my upcoming biopic; Nina Abeysuria for sharing fears; Sarah Standfield for being my copy twin; Sarah Klymkiw for keeping me in check; and Rachel Donati – without whom this book would not exist.

Thanks to Pineapple and Yukari for Japanese and German assistance; and thanks to Guy for trimming my moustache.

Massive thanks to Fern Angel Beattie and Derrick Brown for having faith in – and publishing – a 40-something first-timer with questionable lockdown hair. You completely rawk.

Biggest and most special love to Mum, Dad, Jill, Tom & Elena.

Write Bloody would like to give special thanks to angel donor Sohrab Mehta

ABOUT THE AUTHOR

IAIN WHITELEY has spent the last 18 years writing incognito for creative departments, advertising agencies, newspapers, brands and museums. He's composed board games, billboards, apps, ads, the backs of cereal packets and now poetry, which he took up just before hitting 40. He has a degree in linguistics, an MA in English language, and used to be the voice of a lie detector booth in New York City. This is his first book.

IF YOU LIKE IAIN WHITELEY, IAIN LIKES...

What We Are Given
Ollie O'Neill

This Is How We Disappear
Titilope Sonuga

My Soft Response to the Wars
RC Weslowski

Hard Summer
Francisca Mattos

Counting Descent
Clint Smith

Bloody beautiful poetry books.

Write Bloody UK is an independent poetry publisher passionate
about bringing the voices of UK poets to the masses.
Trailing after Write Bloody Publishing (US) and
Write Bloody North (Canada), we are committed to
handling the creation, distribution and marketing of our authors;
binding their words in beautiful, velvety-to-the-touch books
and touring loudly with them through UK cities.

Support independent authors, artists, and presses.

Want to know more about Write Bloody UK books, authors, and events?
Join our mailing list at
www.writebloodyuk.co.uk

Lightning Source UK Ltd.
Milton Keynes UK
UKHW041358160521
383816UK00001B/96